I0815575

# TUSCAN ROOMS

# TUSCAN ROOMS

## INTERIORS FROM THE HEARTLAND OF THE RENAISSANCE

Photography by
ANTONIO MONFREDA

Text by
AIMEE FARRELL

Introduction by
MARTINA MONDADORI

Essays by
DORA LOEWENSTEIN
CATERINA DE RENZIS SONNINO

CABANA

RIZZOLI
NEW YORK
New York Paris London Milan

CONTENTS

# INTRODUCTION

by MARTINA MONDADORI

Tuscany is not merely a region; it is a living canvas, a dreamscape that has cradled the imagination of artists, poets, and thinkers for centuries. My earliest memories of Tuscany are painted in the warm ochres and soft greens of the hills of Fiesole, just outside Florence. It was here, in this land rich with history, that I first felt the pulse of Italy—the rhythm of its past, present, and future echoing through every stone and cypress tree.

Growing up with my grandmother and her second husband, a proud Tuscan native, my connection to the land was forged not just through history books but through the lived experience of its people, its culture, and its soul. His stories, like the landscapes themselves, were steeped in tradition—of grand villas, olive groves, and vineyards stretching across the undulating hills. The very air here smells of rosemary, sun-drenched earth, and the faintest trace of wood smoke that rises from a hearth inside those ancient homes. Tuscany's historical homes tell stories that no mere guidebook could capture. The houses that dot the landscape—from the stately Medici villas to the more humble yet charming farmhouses—are not simply structures, but symbols of a way of life, a lasting testament to the fusion of architecture, nature, and art. They stand, often framed by rows of meticulously cultivated cypress trees, like silent witnesses to the passage of time, their walls holding the echoes of generations past. But it's not just the architecture that has inspired the world—Tuscany's colors are also a language of their own. The deep russet tones of the Tuscan soil; the soft, sun-washed yellows of the farmhouses; the vibrant greens of vineyards in spring—these are the hues that have inspired countless artists and designers. The light here is like nowhere else: soft, golden, and almost ethereal at dusk, when it stretches across the hills and bathes everything in a tranquil, timeless glow. And just as this light inspired glorious artists over the centuries, it has inspired Antonio Monfreda's work for this book, which captures the essence of *living* in Tuscany through a selection of homes, rooms, gardens, and details. I personally know some of these houses and their inhabitants: memories of garden parties, *aperitivi* under the Tuscan sun, endless conversations over a homemade dinner with a delicious, local red wine. Manfredi della Gherardesca was the epitome of the Tuscan host; he effortlessly gathered friends from around the world at his table in Maremma. He left us too early, and this book wants to be a tribute not only to Tuscany but also to him. And finally, the art. Tuscany is the birthplace of Renaissance art and thought, a place where the boundaries between art, science, and philosophy blurred in a creative explosion that still resonates today. It was here that artists such as Giotto, Brunelleschi, and Donatello revolutionized the world of painting and sculpture, laying the foundations for centuries of artistic innovation. But the legacy of Tuscan art is not confined to the past. It lives on in the contemporary expressions of local artisans, whose crafts carry forward the traditions of their ancestors, weaving history and modernity into a rich tapestry of creativity.

# THE GUARDIANS OF BEAUTY

by **DORA LOEWENSTEIN**

An eye for detail is a rare thing. The beautiful photographs in this book give an insight to this attribute. From beginning to end the images are a feast for the senses. Each one evokes a feeling, whether it is the obvious visual delight, or perhaps the less obvious sensation of the smell of flowers in a vase; the feel of a shiny surface; the sound of footfall on a tiled floor, a pot boiling on a stove, or a ticking clock in the background of a grand parlor in a palazzo. This book is a sensual journey through some of Italy's finest and seldom seen interiors.

Manfredi della Gherardesca and Antonio Monfreda set off on this journey a few years back with a mission to capture the often-forgotten beauty of the palazzos, castles, and villas of Italy's noble families. They wished to share the often-faded grandeur of these much-loved properties, juxtaposed with their noteworthy addresses or grandiose stewardship. The world of modern travel with the all too familiar Four Seasons style is much typified these days, but the beige minimalism and somewhat bland and neutral taste of global brands is not what this book is about. Of course, that aesthetic approach has its place and gives reassuring comfort to many an inveterate globetrotter. But this, *this* is about taste—taste bound in tradition, in family, in history. A pure taste, bolstered by ancient backdrops all captured under the gentle glow of the warm Italian sunshine.

I have a feeling that Antonio and Manfredi had a great deal of fun putting this project together. Visiting their friends, picking the rooms and the spaces to shoot, and then creating the mise-en-scène. There would have been dinners involved and much hilarity while always upholding the highest of aesthetic standards and the greatest of respect to those families and those places in which they were given license to shoot. It is bittersweet then that Manfredi was unable to see the project to completion. My children and I are so happy that Antonio was so determined to see the project put to bed, and it is a huge testament to him and his friendship with Manfredi that he has managed to do so. It cannot have been easy for him to complete, in myriad ways, without his partner in crime. We are also extremely grateful to Martina and all at *Cabana Magazine* who have made this dream become a reality.

I know that Manfredi would ideally have loved to redecorate and repurpose the majority of these houses, as he did with his own. He had such taste, but moreover an endless ability to visualize a better version of a room, a space, a house. So, in the doing of this book, he would have been thinking: "Perhaps that table should be moved;" "That fabric could do with a change—I know a perfect one to replace that faded linen;" "These 18th-century objects would be well offset by a Walton Ford picture;" "Let's add some Rifat Ozbek cushions here." Nothing was ever complete; constant improvements could always be made and nothing to him remained static. Another sadness with his untimely death was that his interior decorating business never really had a proper chance to flourish. This is why I feel that all these thoughts would have been running through his head, while producing this book. He was always forming an opinion of how things should look, and if not changing it, he would have been picking up tips from the houses/rooms he was seeing for the first time. This is not to say he was permanently criticizing what he saw—he was merely trying to improve it. To be fair, perhaps not always, as there was a sharp critical eye that did give way to waspish comments on taste or the lack of it—*de temps en temps!* In the case of this book, and the images that appear within it, I imagine he knew, although his mind would have been whirring, how lucky he was to have such privileged access and would have known that what he and Antonio were seeing and capturing was pretty near perfect anyway.

So, it is with a certain sense of poignancy that I write this small tribute to Antonio and Manfredi. I believe that the pages bear testament to a life lived appreciating beautiful things, most particularly found in people's homes. This book not only shows objects of beauty captured in such aesthetic wonderment but also gives a snapshot into the lives of those who preserve these treasures and live as guardians of such beauty, keeping traditions alive and reflecting a life worth living and the importance of maintaining such things for the generations to come. If Manfredi and Antonio have succeeded in demonstrating this goal, which I think they have, then they have created a fabulous legacy with this wonderful work. *Bravi.*

# TOSCANA FELIX

by CATERINA DE RENZIS SONNINO

We need to start from the landscape.

In Tuscany, from the 1500s to the 1960s, the agricultural system was based on the concept of *mezzadria* (tenant farming). The large estates were subdivided into *poderi* (small farms) with a stable population, which for generations took painstaking care of their allotments, where they knew every corner, every grassy border, clump of dirt or stream of water. This profound relationship with the land implied intense care, alternating different crops and contributing to create the magnificent, harmonious landscape of hills shaped by the work of thousands of peasants, fields, woods, perfect lines traced by rows of cypresses to mark boundaries and pathways with elegant, austere geometry.

The world's biggest garden.

The territory shaped by human beings, with the comforting proximity of others, fosters a reassuring relationship with external reality and nature. The farmhouses scattered amidst these natural geometric lines have grown inside the landscape, in dialogue with it, like the villas, castles, and abbeys that are inserted in a natural way, reflecting an aesthetic sense without excess, since it is the result of laborious, well-measured thought. The familiarity of places has always been a central factor, capable of attracting travelers and curious visitors from all over. We perceive a sense of welcome, also in the most magnificent properties, which are never intimidating but inviting, with discretion, thanks to that proportion based precisely on this sober, concrete temperament, a characteristic aspect of the people here. Houses without bombast, where sedimentation has created a sense of appealing "domesticity" that is, after all, true luxury.

Just as a garden requires time and patience to grow, the same can be said of houses. There's no hurry, because time is more important than man and his urgencies. The houses are harmonious, serene.

The accent on beauty and functionality has produced an agreement reflected both in nature and in architecture. With the Renaissance, the study of perspective and the habit of aesthetic judgment, this sensibility has been further refined, creating a perfect interaction with nature. The artisans—exposed to the landscape, the ideal proportions of buildings, and art—have spontaneously honed their taste, filling their creations with skill and wonder. The Tuscans have invented a landscape in which the buildings blend perfectly with nature. This harmony is not the result of regulations, but of a creative and functional freedom that might seem almost arrogant for its independence. Invention does not display its artifice, and fantasy is refined without ostentation. Apparent simplicity should not be confused with a poverty of ideas, but is the result of elimination of the useless, resulting in elegance. Tuscany has always been "modern," ever since the Renaissance, and it has evolved over time thanks to personalities like the Grand Duke Leopold II, who with infinite farsightedness became the first in the world to abolish capital punishment. With rationality and intelligence, he prepared the manual for the construction of farmhouses and the organization of agriculture, setting the rules and order, thus generating a unified fabric that has then been spontaneously enriched to adapt to the changing needs of families, which expanded their dwellings based on necessities, giving rise to what we now call spontaneous architecture. This respect for unity and harmony has produced a landscape that in spite of changes has conserved its coherence and beauty.

Here there is no court, no apparatus to which to rigidly conform: instead, there is the freedom that permits us to do what is useful and therefore authentic. Seldom have the Tuscans kept up with fashion, until Florence became the capital and many buildings were hastily modified. Intelligent Tuscan thrift has always made it possible to avoid waste: The palaces of the city were renovated, but the objects and knickknacks that were no longer considered suitable were moved to and "rescued" in country houses, creating layers of memories. This reuse has implied the creation of welcoming abodes, where the memories of the owners have settled in an ongoing dialogue between past and present.

Tuscany is also a place of the imagination, the Grand Tour: a collective dream that transcends mere geographical reality. The place of the promise of beauty, culture, history, art, and the good life. It is a powerful dream that attracts us, because it is authentic and does not bend to the desires of the moment. It keeps faith with itself, a place where beauty and understatement mingle, offering a sense of well-being that continues to inspire generations of travelers, artists, and dreamers.

Balance, the gentle and rigorous relationship of measurements and forms, is part of our collective memory, the DNA left to us by brilliant men like Leon Battista Alberti, Paolo Uccello, Brunelleschi, and Piero della Francesca. We have been lucky; now, we should appreciate and preserve this heritage for future generations.

# HILLTOP RENAISSANCE

Thought to be designed by artist and architect Santi di Tito in the mid-16th century, Villa I Collazzi is a refined vision in the Tuscan hills. Distinctive for its double-height loggias, which frame a partially enclosed courtyard, its sparely decorated stone facade is at once imposing—and an exercise in restraint.

"It is a rare beauty," says Bona Marchi Frescobaldi, who, along with her three siblings, inherited Collazzi more than thirty years ago. The villa sits just south of Florence, within a 400-hectare estate encompassing vineyards and olive groves. Its exacting geometry precludes corridors; instead, there is an endless enfilade of rooms, as well as a chapel that houses an untouched Santi di Tito panel painting from 1594.

After Frescobaldi's grandfather Carlo Marchi acquired the house in the '30s as an autumnal country retreat, it remained unfinished. It was Frescobaldi's mother, Elena, who, more than three centuries after the villa's first cornerstone was laid, finally oversaw its completion. And in 1939, she commissioned the landscape architect Pietro Porcinai to install a quartzite and sandstone swimming pool on the rear lawn—still admired for its absolute simplicity. Rather than imposing her own tastes on the interior, Frescobaldi's goal has been to preserve the decorative legacy of her late mother. "We used to call Collazzi her fifth child," she says. Under Frescobaldi's care, it continues to flourish.

SVPPLETVR AB ALTO
NON REVERTETVR
NEC SATIATVR

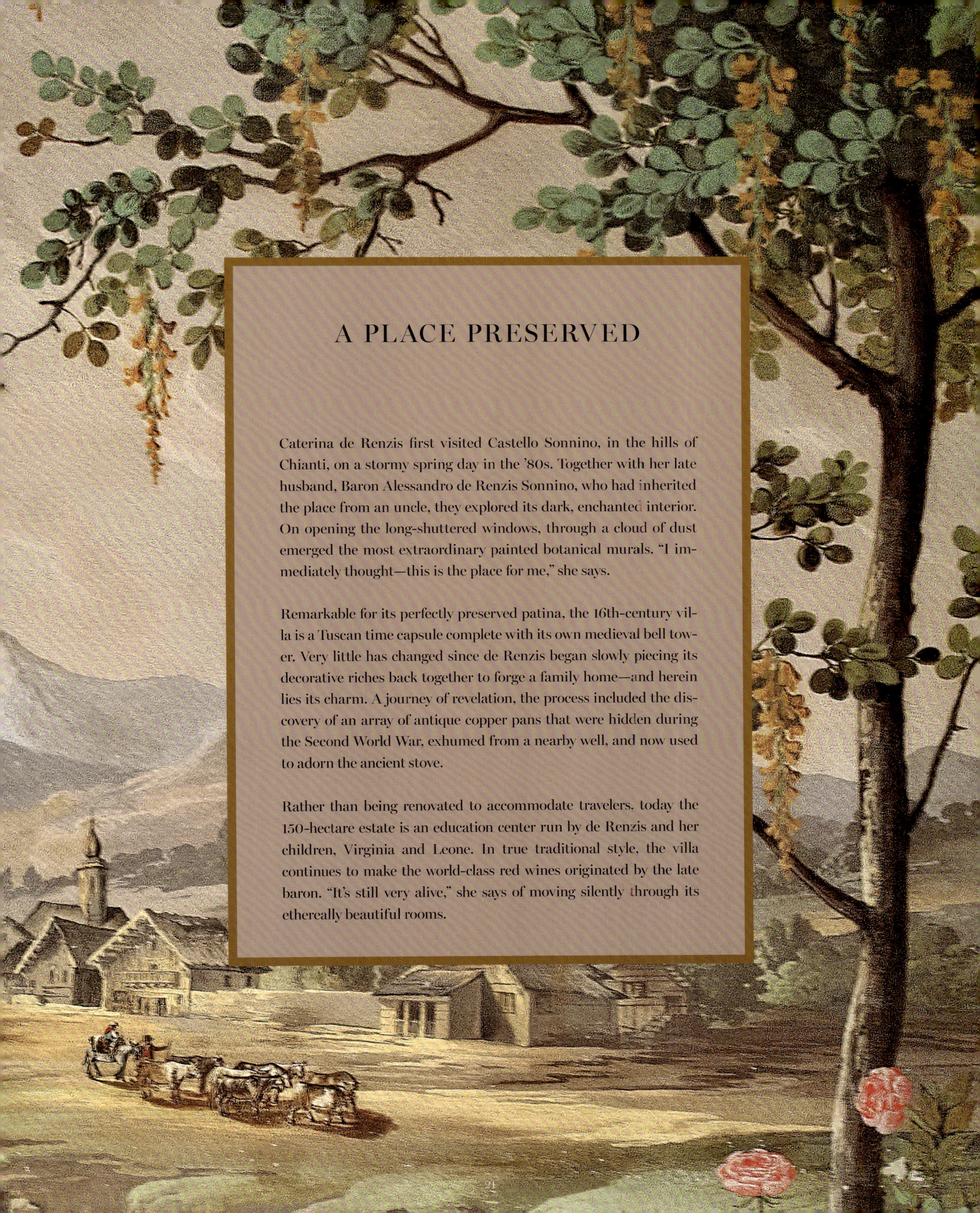

# A PLACE PRESERVED

Caterina de Renzis first visited Castello Sonnino, in the hills of Chianti, on a stormy spring day in the '80s. Together with her late husband, Baron Alessandro de Renzis Sonnino, who had inherited the place from an uncle, they explored its dark, enchanted interior. On opening the long-shuttered windows, through a cloud of dust emerged the most extraordinary painted botanical murals. "I immediately thought—this is the place for me," she says.

Remarkable for its perfectly preserved patina, the 16th-century villa is a Tuscan time capsule complete with its own medieval bell tower. Very little has changed since de Renzis began slowly piecing its decorative riches back together to forge a family home—and herein lies its charm. A journey of revelation, the process included the discovery of an array of antique copper pans that were hidden during the Second World War, exhumed from a nearby well, and now used to adorn the ancient stove.

Rather than being renovated to accommodate travelers, today the 150-hectare estate is an education center run by de Renzis and her children, Virginia and Leone. In true traditional style, the villa continues to make the world-class red wines originated by the late baron. "It's still very alive," she says of moving silently through its ethereally beautiful rooms.

ROOTS
ALEX HALEY

Scritture e Documenti della Cecina 5.
Scritture e Documenti della Cecina 6.
7.
8.
9.
10.
11.
12.
13.
14.
41.
42.
43.
44.
45.
GINORI-LISCI Inventari diversi 1837-1923 46.
Ginori Scritture ed Istrumenti Dall'Anno 1693. al 1694. XXVIII
XXIX
XXX
XXXI
XXXIV
XXXV
LVII
LVIII
LIX
LX
LXI
LXII
LXIII
LXIV
LXV
LXXXV
LXXXVI
LXXXVII
LXXXVIII
XCIII
XCIV
XCV
GINORI-LISCI Documenti
GINORI LISCI Documenti 1930-1933
CRONOLOGICO A.
CRONOLOGICO
CRONOLOGICO B.

# A FIVE-CENTURY-OLD JEWEL

The Ginori family has deep roots in San Lorenzo, having called the Florentine district home for more than seven hundred years. It was Carlo Ginori the Elder, a 16th-century merchant banker trading in wool and silk, who decided to buy a quartet of houses—which came complete with their own orchard—to create what became known as Casa Grande, on Via de' Ginori. Joining together the row of elegant facades, it took four years to complete what is now Palazzo Ginori. Much of the interior was completely remodeled to form a four-story home, built around a porticoed inner courtyard and topped with a loggia with spectacular rooftop views.

While the property is believed to be the work of architect Baccio d'Agnolo, despite its lofty proportions it was originally rather subdued in decoration. Over the intervening years, the sparsely furnished white-walled interior became ever more opulent. This decorative richness reached its apex during the 17th century, when the house was extended and lavishly adorned with everything from Flemish verdure tapestries to the celebrated Doccia porcelain created at the family-founded *manifattura*. The palazzo still holds the power to surprise: the courtyard was recently restored to replicate a 17th-century document found in the family archive, transforming its muted gray columns to their original hue—a bright Pompeian red.

DONATELLO

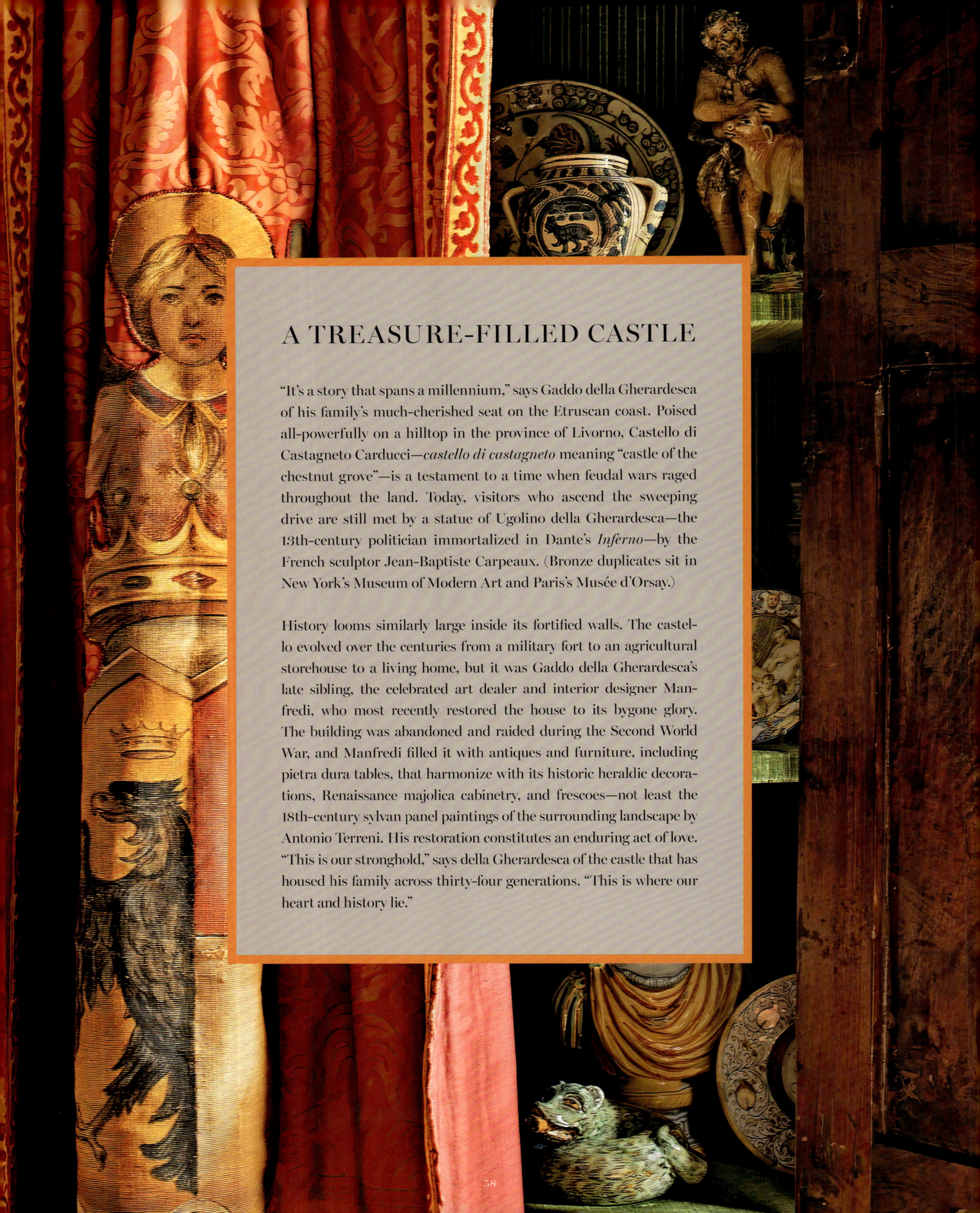

# A TREASURE-FILLED CASTLE

"It's a story that spans a millennium," says Gaddo della Gherardesca of his family's much-cherished seat on the Etruscan coast. Poised all-powerfully on a hilltop in the province of Livorno, Castello di Castagneto Carducci—*castello di castagneto* meaning "castle of the chestnut grove"—is a testament to a time when feudal wars raged throughout the land. Today, visitors who ascend the sweeping drive are still met by a statue of Ugolino della Gherardesca—the 13th-century politician immortalized in Dante's *Inferno*—by the French sculptor Jean-Baptiste Carpeaux. (Bronze duplicates sit in New York's Museum of Modern Art and Paris's Musée d'Orsay.)

History looms similarly large inside its fortified walls. The castello evolved over the centuries from a military fort to an agricultural storehouse to a living home, but it was Gaddo della Gherardesca's late sibling, the celebrated art dealer and interior designer Manfredi, who most recently restored the house to its bygone glory. The building was abandoned and raided during the Second World War, and Manfredi filled it with antiques and furniture, including pietra dura tables, that harmonize with its historic heraldic decorations, Renaissance majolica cabinetry, and frescoes—not least the 18th-century sylvan panel paintings of the surrounding landscape by Antonio Terreni. His restoration constitutes an enduring act of love. "This is our stronghold," says della Gherardesca of the castle that has housed his family across thirty-four generations. "This is where our heart and history lie."

SPLENDOURS OF THE EAST
ARMS AND ARMOUR
PREZZOLINI
PRIMO CONTI
LET THE CHILDREN PLAY

POESIS
HISTORIA

# CHIANTI CLASSICO

The handsome High Renaissance facade of Villa Le Corti, framed by the symmetry of its two towers, is the vision of the talented artist and architect Santi di Tito. When Duccio Corsini and his wife, Clotilde, moved there in the early '90s, they were the first to have lived within its walls for seven decades.

"It had been maintained, but left totally untouched," says Corsini. As well as forging a warm, fully functioning home, where they host cookery classes in the working 17th-century kitchens, they restored its extraordinary triple-tiered cellars. The long, cavernous sequence of rooms and corridors, lined with ancient oak barrels and terracotta jars, is now complete with its own enoteca and osteria, alongside the Renaissance winery.

Perhaps most ambitiously, in 2014 they relocated every one of the twelve thousand documents that comprise the family archive from Florence to a handful of rooms in the San Casciano mansion—now filled to the rafters with accounts, maps, and personal letters that span from the 13th century to the '60s. The walls of one of the grotto-like archive rooms is covered in painterly renderings of rocky forms and symbolic scenes of day and night. The all-encompassing effect is as transportive as the villa's Chianti mountainside views.

# A VERDANT PALAZZO

In 2019, the designer Eva Maria Düringer Cavalli swapped her life in the Tuscan countryside for a palazzo apartment in Oltrarno. Here, the 15th-century walls resonate with the sounds of the bells from the Santo Spirito church just beyond. Set across the entire ground floor, the apartment boasts an expansive garden in central Florence, offering that rarest of city gifts—tranquility. Though a place of respite, it's here that Cavalli hosts a constant procession of friends for coffee, cocktails, informal dinners—and frequent poker nights in the bijou gallery. The sumptuous interiors are layered with modern art, 17th-century furniture, and chandeliers of her own design: a contemporary counterpoint to the stucco, intarsia, and fresco ceiling embellishments. Almost every surface is laden with Cavalli's collection of crystals, semiprecious stones, and spheres, whose elemental surfaces reflect the light that streams in through the large terrace windows throughout the day.

Cavalli's avid collecting is matched only by that of her son Daniele, whose nearby apartment overlooking the Arno is pictured here alongside his mother's. Frequently traveling together to the Parma antiques fair to hunt down treasures to decorate their ever-evolving interiors, the pair have uncannily simpatico tastes.

VOGUE

QUESTA NO.
MA
LUCE
É
SEMPRE

# PRIVATE SPLENDOR

In the shadow of the Cathedral of Santa Maria del Fiore is a rarely glimpsed Renaissance beauty. The Gerini Palace is a trove of art, antiques, and decorative embellishment—from rare glass frescoes to extravagant stucco—that tells the story of four centuries of the Gerini family's collecting and arts patronage.

Originally built at the end of the 1400s, it was reconstructed a century later by Renaissance architect Bernardo Buontalenti, and its rooms filled with spectacular Poccetti frescoes. It was Giuseppe Poggi who gave the palace its final grandiose flourishes; during the 1850s, the acclaimed architect oversaw everything from the rich furnishings and French tapestries down to the lavish door handles.

Marquis Pietro Paolo Cavalletti, the current custodian, has been tirelessly conserving this jewel-box interior together with his mother, Marquise Sveva Cavalletti, ever since inheriting the palace from his granduncle in 1990. Having moved from Milan in 2020, Cavalletti established the palace as his full-time home with wife, Inge, and their two daughters, Camila and Isabella. Though they inhabit the ground floor, occasionally they'll ascend the 18th-century Paoletti staircase to the grandeur of the piano nobile. Camila's wedding party was held amongst the magnificent mirrors of the ballroom, bringing its splendor to vivid life once more.

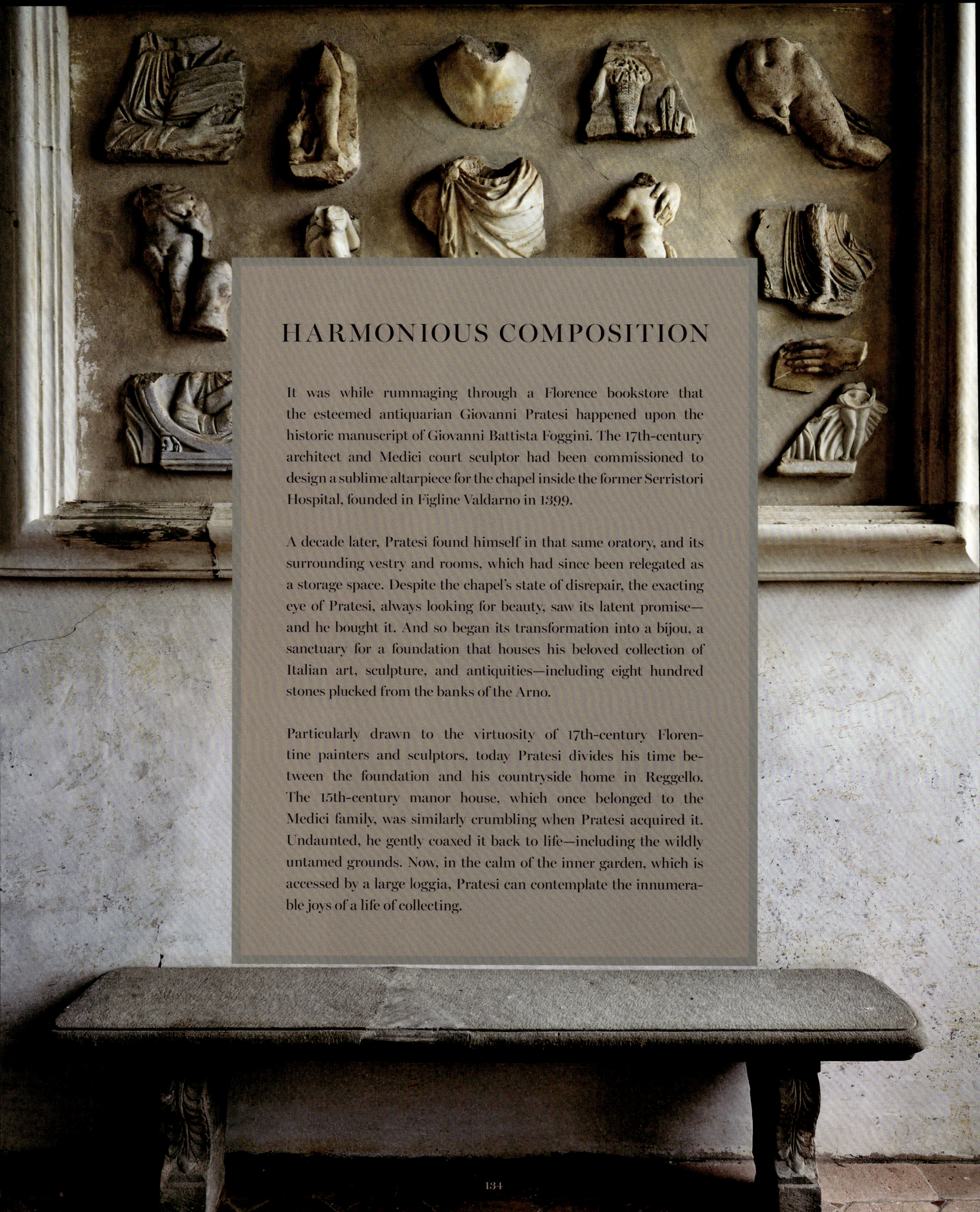

# HARMONIOUS COMPOSITION

It was while rummaging through a Florence bookstore that the esteemed antiquarian Giovanni Pratesi happened upon the historic manuscript of Giovanni Battista Foggini. The 17th-century architect and Medici court sculptor had been commissioned to design a sublime altarpiece for the chapel inside the former Serristori Hospital, founded in Figline Valdarno in 1399.

A decade later, Pratesi found himself in that same oratory, and its surrounding vestry and rooms, which had since been relegated as a storage space. Despite the chapel's state of disrepair, the exacting eye of Pratesi, always looking for beauty, saw its latent promise—and he bought it. And so began its transformation into a bijou, a sanctuary for a foundation that houses his beloved collection of Italian art, sculpture, and antiquities—including eight hundred stones plucked from the banks of the Arno.

Particularly drawn to the virtuosity of 17th-century Florentine painters and sculptors, today Pratesi divides his time between the foundation and his countryside home in Reggello. The 15th-century manor house, which once belonged to the Medici family, was similarly crumbling when Pratesi acquired it. Undaunted, he gently coaxed it back to life—including the wildly untamed grounds. Now, in the calm of the inner garden, which is accessed by a large loggia, Pratesi can contemplate the innumerable joys of a life of collecting.

CONSILIUM
NOSTRUM IN NECESSI
TATIBUS NOSTRIS

CHÂTEAUX EN PAYS DE LOIRE

## FLORENTINE FANTASY

Emanuele Corti Grazzi is inexorably tethered to the grand environs of Palazzo Peruzzi. Constructed on the site of an ancient Roman amphitheater in the heart of Florence, the palazzo is at once majestic and medieval—the oldest parts of the building dating to the 1300s. Corti Grazzi was born inside its storied walls; baptized in its frescoed chapel, which is dedicated to the second apostle of Rome, San Filippo Neri; and—having inherited the house together with his twin sister, Maria Vittoria Corti Grazzi, in the early '90s—still inhabits the enfilade of eight rooms that comprises the piano nobile.

Though the interior serves as a precious testament to the city's all-powerful past, having been built by the Peruzzis, once Florence's wealthiest family, today it is first and foremost a home. "Our house is full of things," says Corti Grazzi of the assemblage of 17th-century treasures, including chandeliers, furnishings, and canvases from artists of the Florentine School, alongside religious artworks, tapestries, and the collection of Etruscan and Roman statuary and archeological treasures passed on from the Peruzzis when his great-grandfather Vittorio Grazzi bought the house around the turn of the 20th century. Occasionally, he'll decamp from the ballroom and the grand galleria, where every inch of wall is filled with frescoes, to the air-conditioned comforts and modern conveniences of a hotel. "But," he says, "it always lures me back."

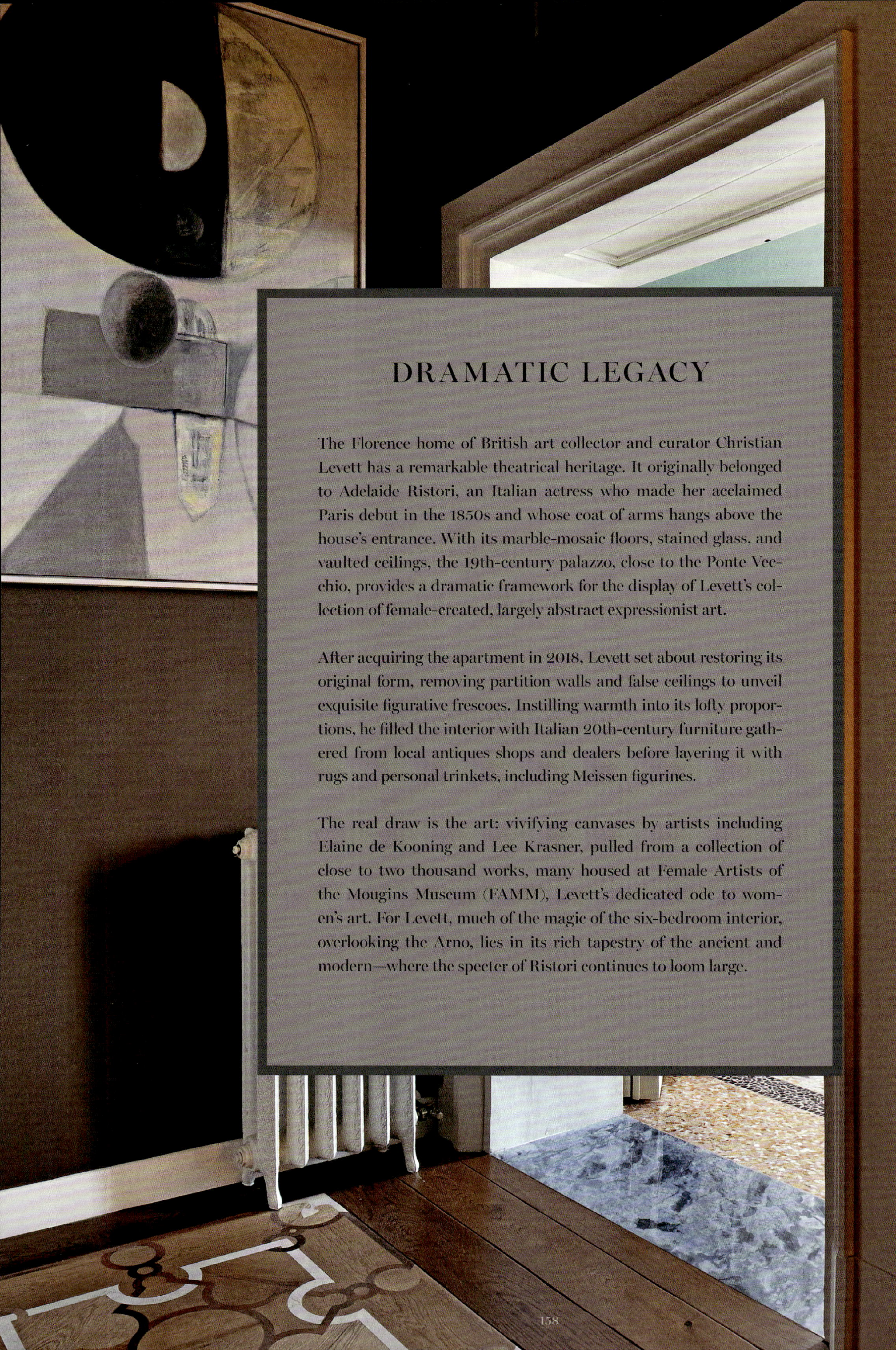

## DRAMATIC LEGACY

The Florence home of British art collector and curator Christian Levett has a remarkable theatrical heritage. It originally belonged to Adelaide Ristori, an Italian actress who made her acclaimed Paris debut in the 1850s and whose coat of arms hangs above the house's entrance. With its marble-mosaic floors, stained glass, and vaulted ceilings, the 19th-century palazzo, close to the Ponte Vecchio, provides a dramatic framework for the display of Levett's collection of female-created, largely abstract expressionist art.

After acquiring the apartment in 2018, Levett set about restoring its original form, removing partition walls and false ceilings to unveil exquisite figurative frescoes. Instilling warmth into its lofty proportions, he filled the interior with Italian 20th-century furniture gathered from local antiques shops and dealers before layering it with rugs and personal trinkets, including Meissen figurines.

The real draw is the art: vivifying canvases by artists including Elaine de Kooning and Lee Krasner, pulled from a collection of close to two thousand works, many housed at Female Artists of the Mougins Museum (FAMM), Levett's dedicated ode to women's art. For Levett, much of the magic of the six-bedroom interior, overlooking the Arno, lies in its rich tapestry of the ancient and modern—where the specter of Ristori continues to loom large.

SCRABBLE
SCRABBLE
ITALIAN DREAM

# WEST TUSCAN HIDEAWAY

In a wilder and less populous corner of the Tuscan coast, amidst some of the region's finest vineyards, sits the charmingly remote Villa Grumolo. Approached via a majestic avenue of pines, and cloistered in Mediterranean-style gardens, the property was originally constructed in the '30s as a shelter for the agricultural workers who tended the surrounding 500-hectare estate.

With its antique rose-color exterior and sage green windows, the building was dramatically remodeled in the '60s. Its latest reinvention happened little more than a decade ago, when the architect Agnese Mazzei was commissioned to open up and brighten the dimly lit lodge, transforming it into a comfortable countryside retreat.

The interior is a deeply personal record of an itinerant life. There are collections of equine art alongside a colorful patchwork of Argentinian and Moroccan carpets, African figurines, and an early 20th-century fireplace repainted in an appropriately rustic and earthy shade.

Devised with communality in mind, its epicenter is the cavernous but cozy sitting room, with oversize sofas and an enormous hearth beneath a broad-beamed, pitched roof. Upstairs, big bathrooms with Tadelakt plaster walls and ochre-hued Indian-stone floors accompany the five intimately sized bedrooms—each one a perfect portal out into the forest of pines below.

TUSCANY
MARKET

## A VISION IMMORTALIZED

For art advisor and interior designer Count Manfredi della Gherardesca, La Civetta was his own deeply personal villa. "It was his place," says Dora Loewenstein. "Something to pass on to his children. A place of absolute freedom." Sequestered on a hilltop in Maremma, in the shade of a pair of vast and ancient oak trees, the farmhouse remains a beloved testament to Manfredi's impeccable taste.

"It's cozy, full of light, and very, very comfortable," says Loewenstein of the interior, a vibrant affirmation of Manfredi's clever eye for color and curios. Put together with signature vivacity and ease, it is an assemblage of the fervent collector's wellspring of objects, from colored glassware to animalistic porcelain and Anglo-Indian furniture and portraiture.

As a designer, Manfredi often composed entire schemes around a single object. Here, blue-and-white porcelain forms the visual springboard for the blue bedroom. "He believed that everything he bought would eventually find a home," says Loewenstein, for whom he built a red clay tennis court in the gardens, originally designed by Arabella Lennox-Boyd. Thanks to Manfredi, La Civetta, with its saturated tangerine exterior, shines beacon-like amongst the one-time marshlands of Maremma.

# A SPECTACULAR SANCTUM

For Andriana Marcello, making her home in Florence's Palazzo Dati Baldovinetti has marked the start of a transformative, new personal chapter. "Living here has been a kind of renaissance," she says of collaborating with architect Agnese Mazzei on the two-year restoration of the elegant 16th-century interior, completed in 2007. Careful to preserve the palace's refined gilded-stucco plasterwork, delicate Romanesque frescoes, and beautiful antique-glass windows, the pair installed parquet floors, a trio of bathrooms, and a modern kitchen.

Decorated with a sense of uninhibited ease, the residence has custom-made Rubelli mirrors and furniture both inherited from Marcello's grandmother and reclaimed from the old chapel that still lies beyond the living room. A keen collector of textiles, she dressed the space with vibrant weaves gathered on trips to Turkey, as well as with jacquards, silks, and finely crafted cloths created by her friend Chiarastella Cattana, the Venetian fabric designer.

Uninhabited for many years, the interior is now imbued with warmth and color. Since Marcello moved in, other friends and family have taken residence on its floors. More than simply a shelter, over the years it has become her sun-drenched sanctuary. Or, as Marcello puts it, her "happy island in Tuscany."

BRUXELLES
l'art de vivre à BRUXELLES

MATER BONI CONSILII

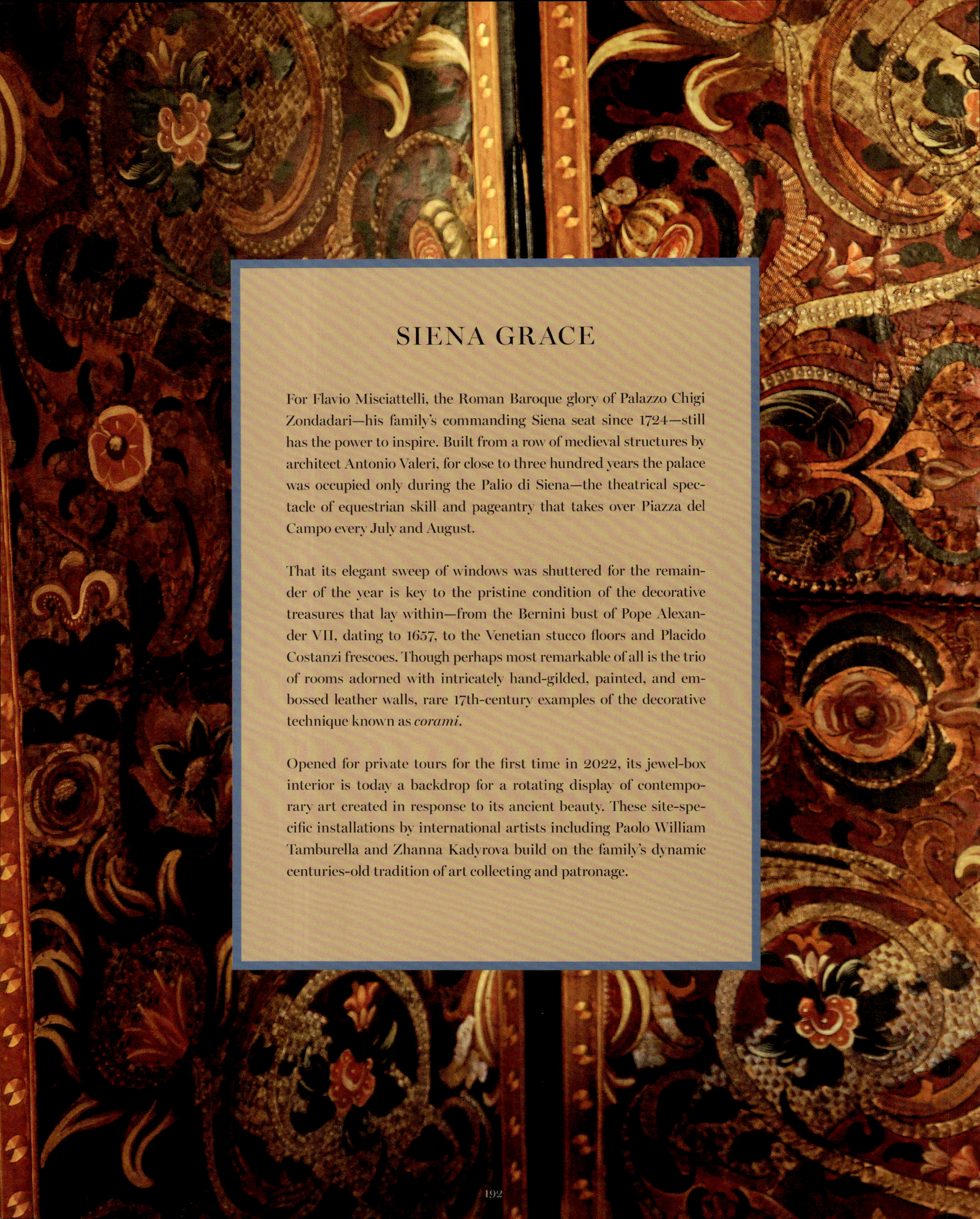

# SIENA GRACE

For Flavio Misciattelli, the Roman Baroque glory of Palazzo Chigi Zondadari—his family's commanding Siena seat since 1724—still has the power to inspire. Built from a row of medieval structures by architect Antonio Valeri, for close to three hundred years the palace was occupied only during the Palio di Siena—the theatrical spectacle of equestrian skill and pageantry that takes over Piazza del Campo every July and August.

That its elegant sweep of windows was shuttered for the remainder of the year is key to the pristine condition of the decorative treasures that lay within—from the Bernini bust of Pope Alexander VII, dating to 1657, to the Venetian stucco floors and Placido Costanzi frescoes. Though perhaps most remarkable of all is the trio of rooms adorned with intricately hand-gilded, painted, and embossed leather walls, rare 17th-century examples of the decorative technique known as *corami*.

Opened for private tours for the first time in 2022, its jewel-box interior is today a backdrop for a rotating display of contemporary art created in response to its ancient beauty. These site-specific installations by international artists including Paolo William Tamburella and Zhanna Kadyrova build on the family's dynamic centuries-old tradition of art collecting and patronage.

FONTE GAIA
BAR
GELATERIA

CHISIAE AC ZONDADARIAE

TIS MONUMENTA

# A KALEIDOSCOPIC PALACE

Laudomia Pucci's earliest recollections of being raised in the splendor of the family's Renaissance palazzo are of glimpsing models swathed in bright Op Art prints as the sounds of applause reverberated from the fashion shows staged beneath her childhood apartment. "To me, this was normal life," she says of the artisanal atmosphere where, in 1951, her father, the politician and designer Emilio Pucci, established his eponymous company—including workshops, fittings rooms, and a boutique—inside the ancestral home.

Remodeled by architect Bartolomeo Ammannati in the 16th century, the ground floor of the Pucci Palace has been transformed into a contemporary tribute to the Pucci family legacy—as seen through Laudomia's innovative curatorial lens. Mannequins adorned in the signature swirls of the Vivara print are displayed cheek-by-jowl with antique marble busts, Murano glassware, and gilded 18th-century furniture and paintings. These experiential archive rooms are daubed in bold shades of fuchsia and Capri blue that nod to the fashion house's palette—a modern counterpart to the romanticism of the interior's Bezzuoli frescoes. "I'm telling the story of what the palazzo has been," says Pucci of the dynamic dialogue between ancient and new. "But also, what it is today—a source of inspiration."

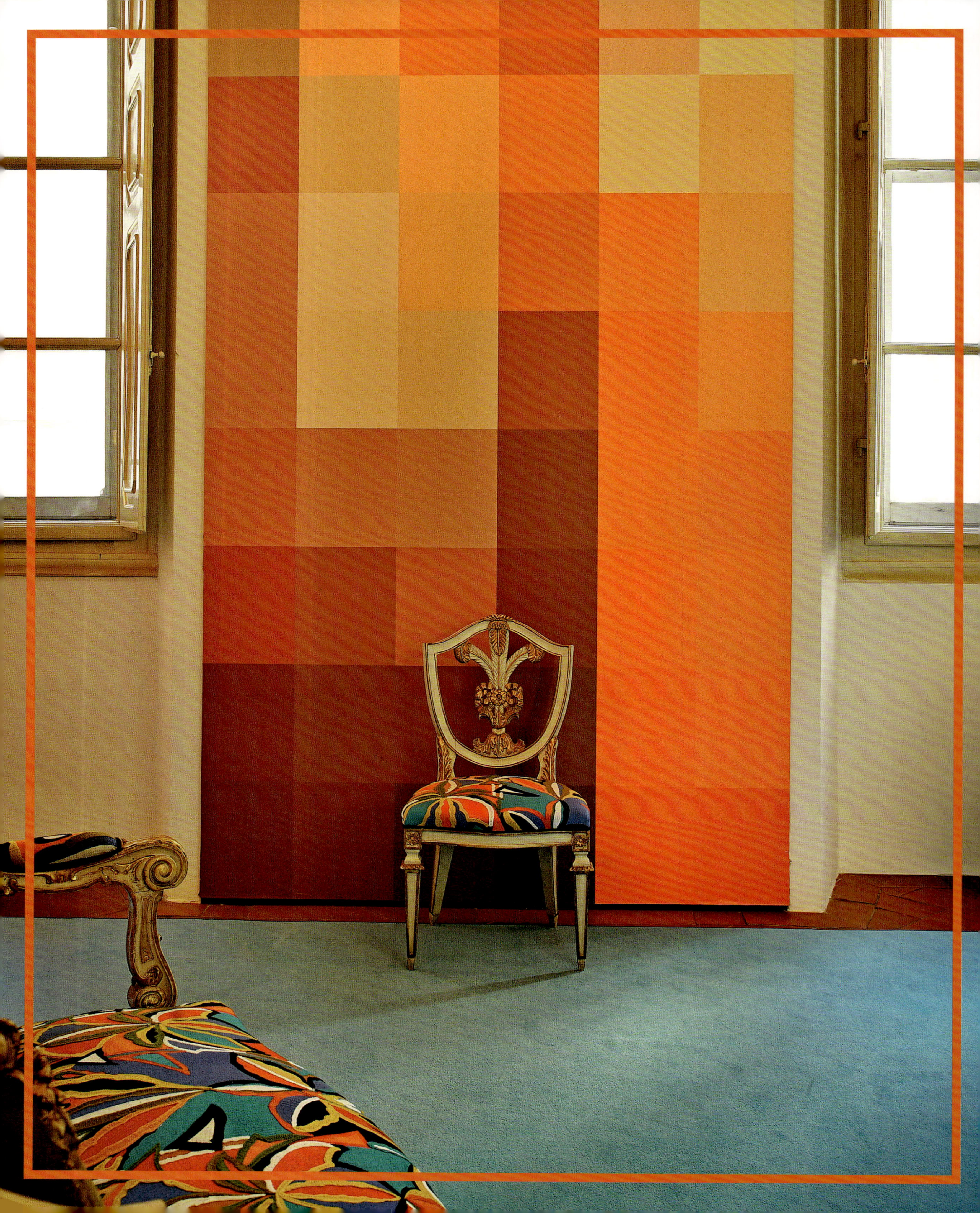

# NATURALISTIC SANCTUARY

Sheltered between green oak forests and the Tyrrhenian Sea lies a bold architectural surprise—the handsome country house of Olmaia. Named for the abundance of elms that once populated the site, the sprawling stone structure sits harmoniously within its natural surroundings.

Though there have been dwellings here for more than five centuries, the house was built by architect Tullio Rossi in 1958, after the owner's previous property nearby was destroyed during the Second World War. The simple exterior is forged with local stone in the style of the hunting lodges of Kenya's Great Rift Valley, with a loggia overlooking long, verdant lawns.

Inside, the rich teak flooring throughout was reclaimed from the *Caio Duilio*, a dismantled Royal Italian Navy warship. Plain white walls provide a serene backdrop to a naturalistic blend of family keepsakes, African curios, historic armor, and antique furniture. The exception is in the dining room, where the flowers on the heirloom Ginori plates that line the walls have inspired an enlivening tangerine palette. The interior's decorative ease suggests a liberated way of living that reflects the untamed beauty beyond the front door. Above it, the poetic words of Gabriele D'Annunzio are inscribed: "Hear the sea in the distance, follow its roar with the murmur of trees."

DI MELE

# UNTAMED FARMHOUSE

Fiona Corsini first laid eyes on her family home, San Giuliano, when it was little more than an assortment of abandoned farm buildings. Set high on a hillside in Florence, close to the Boboli Gardens and surrounded by olive groves, the tumbledown Renaissance structures formed part of the 6-hectare estate of a grand 16th-century villa whose grounds had been a working farm since the medieval era.

"People thought I was crazy," says Corsini of working with architect Themistocle Antoniadis on their metamorphic two-year restoration. Now an Edenic country dwelling in the city, its rose-strewn, green-shuttered facade provides a bohemian shelter for Corsini and her husband, Diego di San Giuliano, and the family's six children and five dogs. The walls are daubed in soft, botanical pigments: in the principal bedroom, a hand-drawn geometric motif, inspired by a medieval pattern seen in Owen Jones's *The Grammar of Ornament*, is overlaid with a *succo d'erba* tapestry bought at auction. Glass cabinets filled with shoes nod to her husband's heritage as the grandson of Ferragamo's founder. By contrast, for Corsini, it has ushered in a new, barefoot way of living closer to nature, perfectly in tune with the passing seasons.

TIZIANO

RISO
ALL'ARTURO
PAPPA AL POMODORO
CROCCANTINI
RISO AL SALTO

# MODERN-BAROQUE MASTERPIECE

The penthouse apartment of Rosella and Carlo Nesi is distinguished both by its preternatural sense of calm and by one of Florence's most preeminent private art collections. Amassed over more than forty years, what began with the acquisition of a Giorgio Morandi landscape has spiraled to span everything from Arte Povera to American Pop Art and Minimalism.

Looking out over the rooftops toward the Duomo and the Fiesole hills that lie beyond it, the apartment is the surprisingly modern crown jewel inside a rare Baroque palace. The uncluttered simplicity of the interior forms the backdrop to an assemblage of painting, photography, and sculpture that lend the air of a live-in gallery.

In the large sitting room, the white walls are punctuated by a pair of Morandis and vivid Lucio Fontana canvases, juxtaposed with a Fausto Melotti sculpture and a self-portrait by the American painter Chuck Close. In the Nesis' hands, even the terrace has been transformed into display space for an installation by Richard Long.

TOR

# ELEGANCE ABRIDGED

"I was looking for a house that would represent me," says architect and interior designer Agnese Mazzei of her hunt for a home in the mid-'90s. An expert in sympathetically reviving heritage interiors, Mazzei discovered the apartment after a long search—and a tipoff from her aunt. Located in the tranquil Florence neighborhood of Santo Spirito, the house has an elegant exterior that veils a grand surprise. Set across two separate buildings, its two halves are connected by a private bridge that stretches across the narrow street below. From the moment Mazzei entered its long enfilade of rooms, she was enraptured.

The residence was built in the 16th century for a family of silk merchants, and Mazzei describes its lofty ceilings, frescoed with Platonic allegories and richly decorative stucco detailing, as more Baroque than Renaissance in style. Carefully preserving the ancient atmosphere, she restored the warm pink and yellow interior, leaving it structurally intact—besides adding a balcony kitchen and stairs to the fourth, mezzanine-level bedroom—and filling it with 17th- and 18th-century furniture.

Bathed in light throughout the day, and with views out onto verdant gardens, the interiors are an enduring source of happiness. "When I come back here after a long day," Mazzei says, "whatever mood I'm in, I change."

NELLE CASE
MILAN INTERIORS 1928–1978
INTERIORS

# SPIRITUAL RECKONING

Despite its deconsecration, the Abbey of San Galgano still holds a sacred and cinematic power. Tuscany's original Gothic church, whose vast solitary form rises skeletal from the rural Siena landscape, is a record of a millennia of myth and mysticism. Built in the 13th century, it is named for Galgàno Guidotti, a feudal knight who renounced his warring ways, established the nearby hermitage after a profound spiritual awakening, and was sainted.

It took seventy years for the community of Cistercian monks who followed in his footsteps to construct the remote rural abbey in his honor. After waves of plague and famine, by the 15th century, it lay empty. While the trio of naves and sixteen pillars that comprise its dramatic cruciform remain—along with the chapter house, scriptorium, and cloister—it has been devoid of a roof ever since the bell tower collapsed in the 18th century.

Close to the abbey stands the Montesiepi hermitage with its Romanesque rotunda. It's here, in the chapel, that Galgàno, who died in 1181, is said to have plunged his sword into a stone after receiving a beatific vision of Christ and his apostles in a round chapel on that selfsame hill. When its blade was recently scientifically scrutinized, the sword was dated to the 12th century.

## A HEALING HOTEL

Claus and Jeanette Thottrup had almost lost hope of finding a Tuscan summer retreat by the time they arrived at Borgo Santo Pietro in 2001. The 13th-century former coaching inn, southwest of Florence, had stood empty for close to thirty years. Despite its ruined state, they were entranced. It sparked a seismic shift in their lives, which saw the Danish couple relocating from London to the secluded village in the Tuscan hills.

"There was just something about the energy," says Jeanette of Borgo. Once a *lazzaretto*—a resting place for the sick—it stands on the medieval pilgrimage trail of Via Francigena. Only an ancient forest lies between the estate and the sacred Abbey of San Galgano.

Jeanette, a onetime fashion designer, has integrated a monastic air into every aspect of Borgo's restorative interior. A hotel since 2008, it has twenty-two beamed and stone-floored rooms layered with Turkish and Persian carpets, reclaimed original Tuscan fireplaces, and flea-market finds, as well as locally custom-made furniture. The 90-hectare grounds, cultivated by the couple over the last twenty years, are the most obviously designed. "The gardens make the rooms," she says. "Not the other way around."

BRINGING TUSCANY HOME
IN TUSCANY

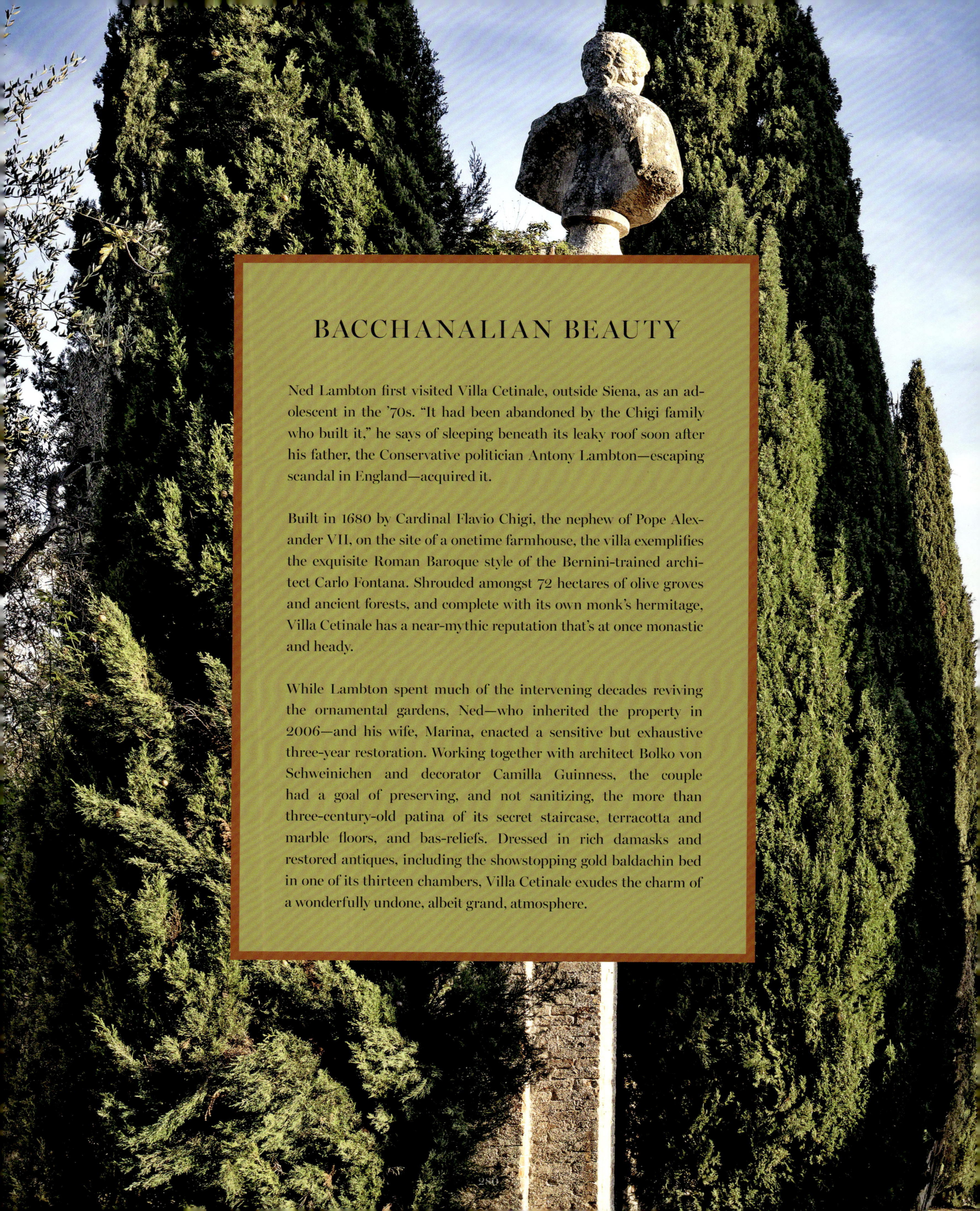

# BACCHANALIAN BEAUTY

Ned Lambton first visited Villa Cetinale, outside Siena, as an adolescent in the '70s. "It had been abandoned by the Chigi family who built it," he says of sleeping beneath its leaky roof soon after his father, the Conservative politician Antony Lambton—escaping scandal in England—acquired it.

Built in 1680 by Cardinal Flavio Chigi, the nephew of Pope Alexander VII, on the site of a onetime farmhouse, the villa exemplifies the exquisite Roman Baroque style of the Bernini-trained architect Carlo Fontana. Shrouded amongst 72 hectares of olive groves and ancient forests, and complete with its own monk's hermitage, Villa Cetinale has a near-mythic reputation that's at once monastic and heady.

While Lambton spent much of the intervening decades reviving the ornamental gardens, Ned—who inherited the property in 2006—and his wife, Marina, enacted a sensitive but exhaustive three-year restoration. Working together with architect Bolko von Schweinichen and decorator Camilla Guinness, the couple had a goal of preserving, and not sanitizing, the more than three-century-old patina of its secret staircase, terracotta and marble floors, and bas-reliefs. Dressed in rich damasks and restored antiques, including the showstopping gold baldachin bed in one of its thirteen chambers, Villa Cetinale exudes the charm of a wonderfully undone, albeit grand, atmosphere.

robot coupe
R 2

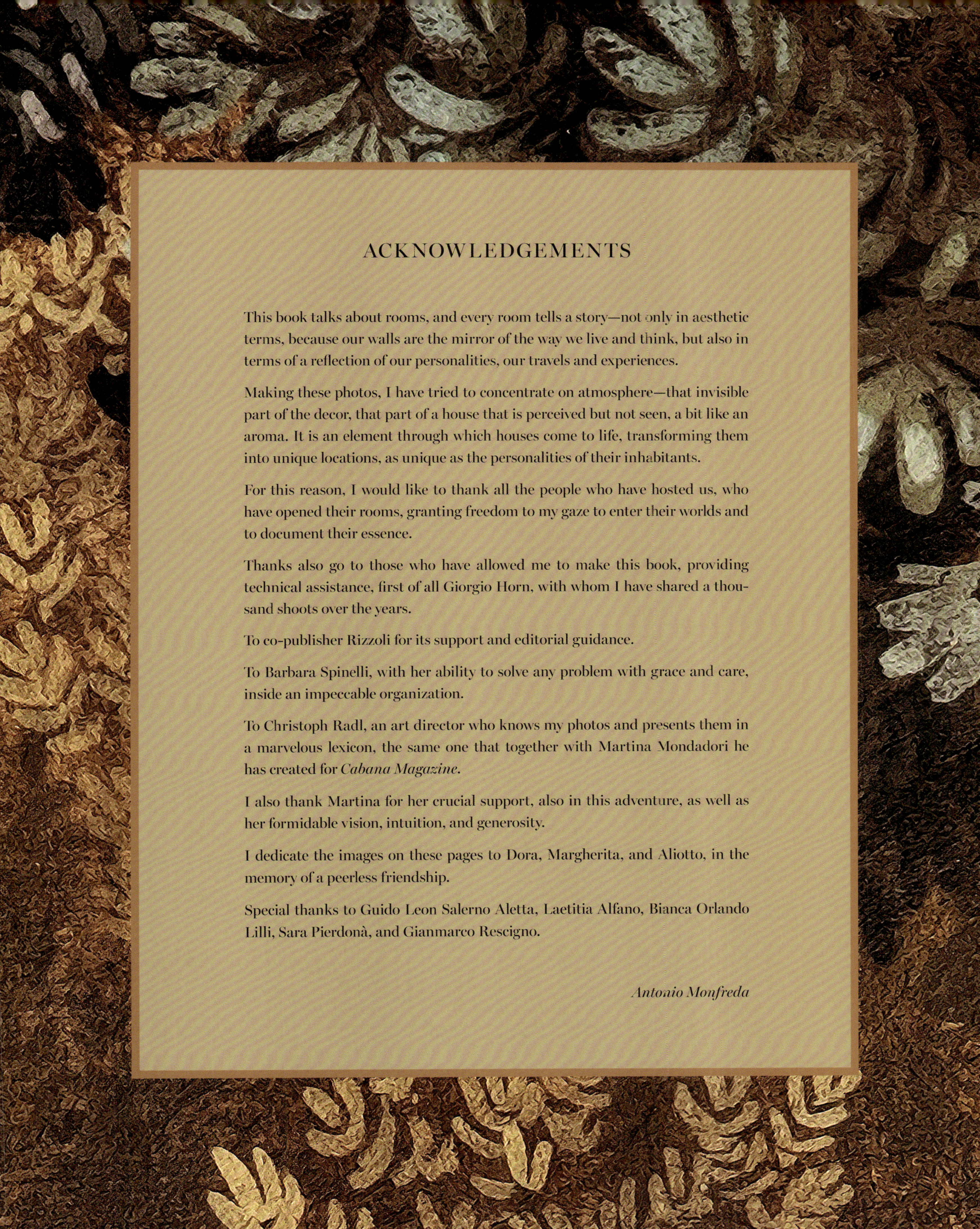


## ACKNOWLEDGEMENTS

This book talks about rooms, and every room tells a story—not only in aesthetic terms, because our walls are the mirror of the way we live and think, but also in terms of a reflection of our personalities, our travels and experiences.

Making these photos, I have tried to concentrate on atmosphere—that invisible part of the decor, that part of a house that is perceived but not seen, a bit like an aroma. It is an element through which houses come to life, transforming them into unique locations, as unique as the personalities of their inhabitants.

For this reason, I would like to thank all the people who have hosted us, who have opened their rooms, granting freedom to my gaze to enter their worlds and to document their essence.

Thanks also go to those who have allowed me to make this book, providing technical assistance, first of all Giorgio Horn, with whom I have shared a thousand shoots over the years.

To co-publisher Rizzoli for its support and editorial guidance.

To Barbara Spinelli, with her ability to solve any problem with grace and care, inside an impeccable organization.

To Christoph Radl, an art director who knows my photos and presents them in a marvelous lexicon, the same one that together with Martina Mondadori he has created for *Cabana Magazine*.

I also thank Martina for her crucial support, also in this adventure, as well as her formidable vision, intuition, and generosity.

I dedicate the images on these pages to Dora, Margherita, and Aliotto, in the memory of a peerless friendship.

Special thanks to Guido Leon Salerno Aletta, Laetitia Alfano, Bianca Orlando Lilli, Sara Pierdonà, and Gianmarco Rescigno.

*Antonio Monfreda*

First published in the United States of America in 2025
by Rizzoli International Publications, Inc.
49 West 27th Street
New York, New York 10001
rizzoliusa.com

Publisher *Charles Miers*
Senior Editor *Philip Reeser*
Production Manager *Alyn Evans*
Design Coordinator *Tim Biddick*
Copy Editor *Claudia Bauer*
Managing Editor *Lynn Scrabis*

Co-published with
Cabana srl
Via Paolo Lomazzo 19
20154 Milan, Italy

Editor in Chief *Martina Mondadori*
Creative Director *Christoph Radl*
Editorial Director *Barbara Spinelli*
Graphic Designer *Giulia Biscottini*
Editorial Coordinators *Laetitia Alfano; Sara Pierdonà*



ISBN: 978-0-8478-4630-6
Library of Congress Control Number: 2025931538

Printed and bound in Italy by Nava Press srl
2025 2026 2027 2028 / 10 9 8 7 6 5 4 3 2 1

The authorized representative in the EU for product safety and compliance is
Mondadori Libri S.p.A.
via Gian Battista Vico, 42
20123 Milan, Italy
mondadori.it